This Notebook Belongs To

____

Made in the USA
Monee, IL
13 December 2021

85246293R00070